**PLANNING
YOUR
PHD**

T0286198

POCKET STUDY SKILLS

*Series Editor: **Kate Williams**, Oxford Brookes University, UK*
Illustrations by Sallie Godwin

For the time-pushed student, the *Pocket Study Skills* pack a lot of advice into a little book. Each guide focuses on a single crucial aspect of study giving you step-by-step guidance, handy tips and clear advice on how to approach the important areas which will continually be at the core of your studies.

Published

14 Days to Exam Success
Blogs, Wikis, Podcasts and More
Brilliant Writing Tips for Students
Getting Critical
Planning Your Essay
Planning Your PhD
Reading and Making Notes
Referencing and Understanding Plagiarism
Science Study Skills
Success in Groupwork

POCKET STUDY SKILLS

Kate Williams

Emily Bethell Judith Lawton Clare Parfitt
Mary Richardson Victoria Rowe

PLANNING YOUR PHD

BLOOMSBURY ACADEMIC

LONDON • NEW YORK • OXFORD • NEW DELHI • SYDNEY

BLOOMSBURY ACADEMIC
Bloomsbury Publishing Plc
50 Bedford Square, London, WC1B 3DP, UK
1385 Broadway, New York, NY 10018, USA
29 Earlsfort Terrace, Dublin 2, Ireland

BLOOMSBURY, BLOOMSBURY ACADEMIC and the Diana logo
are trademarks of Bloomsbury Publishing Plc

First published 2010 by PALGRAVE
Reprinted by Bloomsbury Academic, 2022

A catalogue record for this book is available from the British Library.

A catalogue record for this book is available from the Library of Congress.

ISBN: PB: 978-0-2302-5193-9
ePDF: 978-1-1370-1374-3

Printed and bound in Great Britain

To find out more about our authors and books visit
www.bloomsbury.com and sign up for our newsletters.

Contents

About the authors

Kate Williams manages Upgrade, the Study Advice Service at Oxford Brookes University, UK. She has worked with students from Foundation to PhD level and has written a range of books and materials on study skills. She is series editor of the Pocket Study Skills series

Emily Bethell completed her interdisciplinary PhD in Biology, Anthropology and Psychology in 2009 and now works as a Senior Lecturer in Primatology and Animal Behaviour at Liverpool John Moores University, UK.

Judith Lawton is Former Deputy Head of Hounslow Language Service and English as an Additional Language consultant. She has undertaken doctoral research in bilingual learner education and has 40 years of experience in teaching and teacher training.

Clare Parfitt-Brown is a Senior Lecturer in Dance at the University of Chichester, UK. Her PhD focused on the history of the cancan and led to ongoing research into the cultural histories of popular dance practices.

Mary Richardson completed an ESRC-funded PhD investigating the assessment of Citizenship Education in 2008. She is now a Senior Lecturer in Education at Froebel College, Roehampton University, UK and continues to develop research in the areas of both assessment and citizenship education.

Victoria Rowe works as a piano teacher for many years prior to completing her PhD in 2008. She is currently a Teaching Associate at the University of Sheffield, UK and also works as a freelance researcher.

Acknowledgements

Our thanks to the many people who have contributed to this book. Some will see their contributions directly reflected in the text: some researchers will see echoes of their work here, and our reviewers will see their comments. Others may not see their contributions directly – the many research students who attended Kate's workshops over the years at the University of Oxford, Oxford Brookes University, and most of all at Roehampton University – but their insights and strategies form the bedrock of this book.

Particular thanks to our critical reviewers for their observations and specific suggestions:

Gordon Clark (FBA), Halford Mackinder Professor of Geography, University of Oxford, who provided many thought-provoking discussions and critical comments

Penelope Cave, harpsichordist and 1st-year PhD student in musicology

Dr Anthony Dyson, artist and writer in art; PhD supervisor in the Department of Art and Design, Institute of Education, University of London

Dr Hywel Dunn-Davies, recent PhD graduate in artificial intelligence

Dr David Evans, Head of Graduate School, Oxford Brookes University

Dr John Haigh, former Principal Lecturer in Chemistry, Sheffield Hallam University

Dr Damien Hall, Research Assistant on the Accent and Identity on the Scottish–English Border project, University of York

Professor Michael Hitchcock, Deputy Dean for External Relations and Research, University of Chichester

Dr Mandy Holmes, Senior Lecturer in Psychology, Roehampton University

Jenny Kendrick, MA, a current PhD student

Jennifer McClean, a writer, who has helped both her children through PhDs

Dr Tristan McCowan, Lecturer in Education and International Development, Institute of Education, London

Dr Adam Moss, petrophysicist, London

Dr Pat Pinsent, Senior Research Fellow, Roehampton University, London

Dr Richard Race, Co-Director of Postgraduate Training Scheme, School of Education, Roehampton University

Dr Marion Ross, formerly Dean of Mills College, California, and Professor of Economics, USA

Thanks too to Sallie Godwin for capturing the spirit of our intentions in her astute illustrations.

Introduction

How this book happened

The idea for this guide arose at the end of one of Kate's PhD writing workshops. In the pause before everyone headed for the door, the recognition of the sum total of the expertise in the room hung over the table. Some of us had already achieved the doctorate and had rejoined the group to share experiences of the final lap; others were close to completion. By the time you read this, we will all have 'Doctor' before our names – except Kate, who has watched our journeys over many years.

The participants in the workshops came from many disciplines across the Arts, Social Sciences and Science – in fact the better workshops had the greatest range of disciplines. This ensured that we could never take shortcuts in our thinking or explanations or lapse into the jargon of the subject. It made us focus on the shared core of the research process, appreciate issues in other disciplines, and struggle to articulate complex ideas in simple language and diagrams. We could then draw on this clarity when we returned to the complexity of our own research.

The authors' research fields are within dance, education and science. We have maintained our contacts with workshop companions in other fields, and shared this script with reviewers in the UK and the USA. We are confident that there will be something here for you, and that the simple framework and clear language will allow your complex ideas to flourish, as it did with us.

Who is the book for?

This guide is for anyone thinking about, or involved in, the early stages of research work. You may:

▶ be thinking about the practicalities of starting a research project or a PhD – take a look at Part 1

▶ be pondering the transitions you will have to make, personal and academic, if you do decide to pursue the research avenue – look at Parts 2 and 3

▶ have started your research, and be at one of the many points where you need to focus or refocus your research question – try our Workshop in Part 4

▶ need to write a research plan, upgrade, proposal or critical review, and need some starting points – see Part 5.

You may not yet be thinking about conferences or publication (Part 6), but that is precisely why it is here – it is something you do need to think about from early on in your life as a researcher.

What is the book about?

Flick through, dip in and have a look. You do not have to read this book from start to finish (although it is so short that you can). Its starting point is the things we wish we'd known about from the outset, such as:

- selecting the right university, research group and supervisor for you (pp. 12–18)
- opportunities for both small- and large-scale funding (pp. 8–11)
- how the outline of your planned research in your initial application is the first of many research plans (pp. 17–21 and 89–95)
- how different a project of at least three years is from a three-month project
- how it can change your work/life balance (pp. 32–4)
- how important it is to maintain a network of friends, both fellow research students and those outside academia.

This book goes beyond this list, and we hope you will find it a useful point of reference well into your PhD. Of course, if you started your PhD journey knowing everything that you would find out along the way, there would be no point in setting off. But learning from those who have travelled the path already can make the journey easier and quicker.

'To know the road ahead, ask those coming back' (Chinese proverb)

And finally – we now know that a PhD is a stepping stone, not a finishing line. It does not need to be perfect, just good enough to move on to the next stage, whatever that may be.

About this guide

Part 1 Deciding to do a PhD is about the conscious exploration and decision making you need to engage in during the application process.

Part 2 Getting started offers pointers to those first days and weeks as a PhD student.

Part 3 Becoming a researcher is an introduction to some of the key relationships, considerations and skills you will develop in the first few months of your PhD and beyond.

Part 4 The Workshop – Mapping your research process is where we invite you to take part in the practical thinking exercises we undertook in the early stages of our PhDs. Here you clarify your thinking and sharpen your focus on your research question.

Part 5 Writing research plans gives guidance on how to approach the research planning you will be required to do in the early phases of your PhD (particularly the introduction and the literature review).

Part 6 Finding audiences for your research takes a brief look at the planning you need to do right from the beginning to communicate your research through seminars, conferences and publications.

Something may have caught your interest from a personal or professional experience, or intrigues you from previous study – and this has become the focus for your PhD.

Your interest might be quite precise-looking ...

- ▶ heritage language learning with Chinese children in the UK
- ▶ forensic linguistics – the language of the police
- ▶ the effect of exercise on the vertebral column in the elderly
- ▶ computational modelling of fuel cells
- ▶ history of the Comédie-Française: scrutinising the links between British and French theatre
- ▶ development of methods to assess the physiological, behavioural and psychological aspects of animal welfare

or very general …

- artificial intelligence
- urban change in Russia
- Canadian water politics
- outsourcing and global software.

Whatever it looks like now, it will change. When you start reading different literature you'll discover a whole new world of arguments and findings which will present you with all sorts of directions and options. You will – through the process of developing your argument – narrow it down to a question that is researchable. It will continue to evolve in small ways until you become a 'Doctor' in your specialist field.

But all this lies ahead. Right now your priority is to find your research opportunity, the right community of expertise, the right supervision, the pattern of study and form of doctorate that suits you, and indeed the funding to allow you to pursue it. This is what this section is about.

2 What kind of PhD?

The PhD ('Doctor of Philosophy' whatever your subject) is traditionally a minimum 3-year period of full time study, by the end of which you will have produced an extended piece of writing, typically in the range of 60,000–100,000 words. This 'thesis' is an apprentice piece that demonstrates your capabilities as a researcher at the highest level. It will present new knowledge and demonstrate an important contribution to your subject area. Examiners who are highly qualified in your field (usually one internal, one external) assess the thesis and, if it is acceptable, and you are able to defend it in an oral examination (a viva), you are awarded a PhD.

The 'big book' approach is not the only way to gain a PhD. People are now able to demonstrate the qualities of 'doctorateness' in a variety of ways in both process and format.

4-year full time (equivalent)
A 4-year PhD may include a number of research training modules in the first year, followed by three years of research.

Linked with a Master's programme (a '1+3')

A 1-year Master's + 3 years' PhD, or a 2-year Master's + 2 years' PhD. Taking some Master's modules might be an option if you have gaps in your knowledge or require specialist training. The 'upgrade' after the first year of PhD study is a point of decision – to continue with the PhD, or leave with a Master's.

PhD by publication

This requires a number of articles (typically three or four) to be published in peer-reviewed journals. It is particularly well suited to people already in the academic world who have published.

The professional doctorate

Qualifications such as the EdD or PsychD are based on the candidate's own professional practice. It may take the form of 5 years' part time study (less with some full time study): typically with taught input in the first 2 years, followed by a research proposal. The final thesis is usually around 40,000 words.

Practice-based PhD

These are becoming increasingly common in the creative and performing arts and design. A substantial part of the research process and output takes the form of artistic or design practice, for example choreography, visual art, music or media production. Innovative formats for research can sometimes be accommodated, depending on the university department. A written submission of around 30,000–60,000 words that contextualises or reflects on the practice is also usually required.

One doctorate sponsored by the National Trust involved researching a collection of music in a country house, writing about it and performing and lecturing on it.

Participants in our workshops have followed all these formats, from the traditional to the innovative practice based and everything in between!

Full time or part time study may be a matter of choice, or it may be determined by your circumstances. Consider whether you …

▸ can afford to study full time – or is it just not possible? If you do not have funding (see p. 8), how will you manage?

▸ have an end date in mind? And is it realistic? Figures from HEFCE (Higher Education Funding Council for England) will give you an idea of the variation between different universities and departments.

▸ have something (or someone) to place a specific deadline on your completion?

> Of all PhD students who enrolled in 1999–2000, 75% of full time and 35% part time students had completed within 7 years. (HEFCE 2007)

Both ways of studying for a PhD result in the same end, but they are very different experiences.

If you choose part time …

▸ how will you feel about getting stuck into your books after a long day's work, over your weekends, or during your precious annual holiday? 'Part time' can feel very full time in reality – and you can feel more isolated.

But then ... many part timers describe the PhD as a wonderful distraction from other parts of their life.

If you choose full time ...

▶ the PhD will become a large part of your identity for a long time and it can be difficult to escape from it.

But then ... many full timers argue that being able to immerse themselves in the process is a luxury only full time study can offer.

Your decision. Between us, we did all of the above: we completed our PhDs by full time and part time routes – some full time years, some part time – some with months/years off, and extensions. But we did get there!

You have an idea that excites you. You now need to ask yourself, 'Can I afford to do this?' and then ask, 'Can I afford *not* to do this?' You could just say 'No' to the first question, and forget the whole idea. But it's more difficult to ignore the second ... So, where do you start?

Apply for an advertised post

The most straightforward way to fund your PhD is to apply for a fully funded advertised PhD. You can sign up to online sites and they will send you weekly updates of advertised PhDs (see p. 119).

Note that:
- Competition is high, and the likelihood of finding an advertised post that fits with your research idea will vary according to your area of interest.
- You need to be flexible: a funded PhD has already been through a competitive process to secure the funding, so the project is likely to be a good one. Being flexible in your approach may be a small price to pay for having your fees paid direct and receiving a monthly bursary.

Apply for your own Research Council funding

You can apply for your own funding from one of the seven Research Councils (RCs) (see p. 119). Together, these are the biggest funders of postgraduate work in the UK. Here you need to:

▶ apply in collaboration with your proposed supervisor/department (it is in the university's interest to support you). Note that the application will require a lot of time

▶ make your proposal relevant to the RC's priorities

▶ write a substantial part of your research proposal *prior* to getting the funding – so you need to have a well-developed research idea.

The total figure of funds available to support research varies between RCs, and fluctuates. The introduction of the Research Excellence Framework (REF) in 2013 means that RCs now look for:

▶ impact statements – the impact your research might have on potential users of the research

▶ greater involvement of stakeholders in the design and dissemination of the outcomes

▶ increasing inter- and multidisciplinary research, where groups of specialists come together to work on complex issues or problems (see pp. 56–9).

Apply for funding from other bodies

Additional funding bodies include research charities such as the Wellcome Trust, the Leverhulme Trust and the Association of Medical Research Charities. Other (smaller) funding sources are out there, usually tailored to specific groups (e.g. to fund women in science). Explore:

▸ PhD studentships funded by the university itself from internal research funds: your potential supervisor may be able to submit an initial application for funding on your behalf (and check towards the end of the financial year in case there are any unspent funds)

▸ funding guides listing charities that support postgraduate work – available free at your local library

▸ your contacts: do you know anyone who has funding? How did they get it? Can they advise you on applications?

Or just start searching and see what you can find.

Self-funding

A PhD is an enormous financial commitment. If you plan to self-fund you need to be realistic and budget carefully. Find out:

▸ the full cost of fees so you know what you are dealing with (including extra charges

for bench fees, materials and so on) – and anticipate rises in future years
- whether additional funds are available (e.g. small grants, conference funds).

If you start off self-funding it can be hard to attract funding later in your PhD. Self-funding may, however, allow you more flexibility in research topic and completion dates.

Extra cash

Research Councils encourage you to work as a lecturer or similar whilst you study. (But do be disciplined: employment at university is not the same as research time.) Consider:

- working as a research assistant on other funded research – you pick up experience along the way
- registering at your institution's Human Resources (HR) department for casual work, e.g. transcription, data entry, note taking, marking, invigilation. You have skills other people need.
- seeing if family or friends are able to help.

The decision about where you do your PhD will be based on a balance of considerations: the opportunity, supervisor, department, university, town/city, country. Some of us are tied to one geographical location (family, work commitments): for others the world is our oyster. The key drivers are the funded research project, the supervisor, and the research centre or department.

The advertised PhD post

Most institutions and departments select research students whose interests match their funded projects and complement the research strengths of their team. The project will lead you to a particular department and supervisor.

Choosing a department/research centre

Some departments will indicate that they are willing to consider expressions of interest in inter- or multidisciplinary areas, conscious that they may be able to offer two, or even three, supervisors. The relevant university webpages will show this, and may list broader subject areas within which your idea may fit.

From a distance you can check out:

▶ **Research Assessment Exercise (RAE)** or (from 2013) the Research Excellence Framework (REF) score: what reputation does the university (or, more importantly, department or research group) have nationally and internationally in your subject area? Good departments will advertise their RAE score on their websites. As with all league tables – read between the lines.

▶ **Size** of the body of research students in the department. Some points in the RAE score are allocated simply on the size of the body of research students. A large group of research students might compel the institution to devote resources to them, but a small group of research students may allow for a more individual approach.

▶ **PhD completion figures** published by HEFCE (see p. 6) are a useful indicator of how much support PhD students receive, but these can be very subject specific so drill down to your department.

- **Departmental webpages:** Staff profiles? Evidence of departmental research activity? Are there regular discussion groups or seminars? Do PhD students present papers at these?
- Is there a **Doctoral Training Programme** offering enhanced training in collaborative work?

On the ground you can check out:
- **Facilities** on offer to PhD students (lab/studio/work space/conference funds).
- **Funding and support** (see p. 8–11)
- **Library and departmental resources** – are the journals that cover your subject available in the library or online?
- **Research group activities** (both academic and social) on notice boards.
- **Extra-curricular activities** – will you be able to access the cultural and other (e.g. sporting) activities you enjoy in or around the university?

Choosing your supervisor

Choosing your supervisor is one of the most important decisions you will make in planning your doctoral work. A PhD is not a solo project but a training course for researchers, and many students underestimate the level of negotiation and collaboration involved. Your supervisor may influence the topic of your PhD, the methodology you choose, what you publish during your PhD and in whose name, which conferences you attend and present at, and, ultimately, your job.

Groundwork

▶ Read the work of any potential supervisor, and if possible, talk to them.
▶ Talk to their current/past PhD students.

Consider these options

▶ A supervisor in your current institution whom you already know, versus a new supervisor, possibly in another institution, who may offer a new perspective.
▶ A young, enthusiastic but inexperienced supervisor, versus an older, busier, but more experienced supervisor.
▶ Supervisors whose skills/styles/levels of experience complement each other, versus supervisors with similar interests.
▶ The supervisory 'team' – all those involved in your progress whatever their titles: 'Director of Studies', 'Co-supervisor'.

When you feel you are getting close to what you are looking for, have an email exchange – or meeting – with a possible supervisor to establish exactly what you both have to offer. Remember, it is a two-way street: your supervisor is also choosing you.

Questions to ask your supervisor

▶ How often will we meet?
▶ How will my progress be monitored?
▶ Are you contactable all year round (for example, not off on remote fieldwork), and what is the typical turnaround time for feedback on submitted work?
▶ What is your approach to publication during the PhD?
▶ Will you support/help me to look for an academic post after the PhD?

It may, of course, turn out quite differently and be fine – but for now, you need to clarify your expectations.

Questions to ask yourself

▶ How independent do you like to be? Will your supervisor support this?
▶ Which methodological approach do you prefer? Does your supervisor advocate this approach?
▶ What sort of feedback do you benefit most from (critical/constructive/ encouraging)? Does your supervisor offer this?
▶ Are they really interested in your topic, and in you as able to tackle it?
▶ Do you get on with your potential supervisor?

When you have explored these possibilities you are ready to make an initial application. Follow the instructions and format provided by the institution meticulously. Incomplete applications will not be considered at all.

The two things you need to focus on are:
1 What the university/department is looking for in a research student.
2 How you can demonstrate these attributes.

The university is looking for …

… a clear summary of what you want to do, and why it is important. They want to see evidence that you:

- know how to develop a line of logical argument
- are able to communicate ideas in a clear and concise manner
- know the relevant literature to consult (to begin with, at least)
- are proposing a realistic and achievable project
- have the skills which make you the obvious person to do this project.

Try to show that you are aware of the different types of output that will be expected of you – publications, conference presentations and, where relevant, plans to bring in extra money to support your research.

We are wary of stereotyping the characteristics that are sought in the different disciplines, but feel that there are some generalisations that make a useful starting point. If you can place yourself on the spectrum opposite, it may help you think about what the university will be looking for in your application.

	Science	Technology	Social sciences	Humanities	Arts
First degree ...	... in the discipline			... more flexibility in subject area	
Application places importance on ...	... specific subject knowledge			... personal statement	
Approach developed through ...	... skills in field/lab/ practical setting			... a reflective process	
Project developed ...	... to fit research group focus			... in creative partnership with supervisor(s)	

Don't worry that you will be held to this initial statement of interest: supervisors know that the focus will change as your question becomes more focused. They are more interested now in how you think – and write.

How you demonstrate these qualities

Evidence of previous written work

You may be asked for this – typically from your undergraduate studies or Master's dissertation. Your proposed supervisor will advise on what kind of work to send. Make sure it is something that showcases your writing skills to their best.

Curriculum vitae

Update your CV to make it look more like an academic CV. Many academics post their CVs online. Look at the kinds of information they provide, and think about your own achievements. You may not have publications to list, but are you a member of any relevant societies? Did you gain any specialist training during your undergraduate degree? Did you raise money or gain funding for any projects? Make sure you list any expertise or experience that may be useful for the PhD so that your potential supervisor can see your suitability for the role or post.

Letters (or emails) of recommendation from academics who know you

Make sure you ask potential referees if they are happy to do this *before* you give their names to potential supervisors or universities you are applying to. If you are not a native speaker of English you will be required to show evidence of your language level. US universities also expect a Graduate Record of Examination (GRE).

The result?

If you do well, you will be invited for interview, by phone or videolink if you live in another country. We all had very different experiences of our PhD interviews. Some were highly formal; others felt relaxed and informal. So much of the interview process relies on first impressions and personal interactions that we will not talk about this here … other than to say 'Good luck!' with this stage of your journey.

Part 2 picks up a little further along the path: when you arrive at your institution as a PhD student.

The decision to study for a doctorate is unlike any academic decision you have taken before. Your undergraduate degree may have been a semi-automatic choice or a necessary life-changing one; a Master's degree offers a relatively high return (in terms of academic boost and employability) for a relatively small investment of time and effort ... but a PhD?

Is a PhD really for you?

Take a moment to consider the reasons for *not* doing a PhD. This bulleted list may seem a little blunt or simplistic, but do pause and glance at it. Taking the plunge before you are ready may lead to disappointment – yours or other people's.

You might question if a PhD is for you if you:

▶ do not know what else to do

▶ want to boost your prospects in the job market generally (as opposed to having a specific aim of working where a PhD is essential, such as in a research environment or university, in policy or consultancy)

▶ are not really committed to the idea but feel under pressure from others.

And here's a tough one:

▶ if you cannot afford it, cannot find funding, or are really overstretched with other commitments.

Yes? No? Remind yourself – why do a PhD?

You need to have good reasons for investing this huge amount of time, effort and money into a single project, and you need to know what these reasons are.

You need to be:

▶ passionate about a particular subject
▶ self-motivated and love learning new things
▶ enjoy and excel at new projects.

Ultimately, you want to:

▶ further your knowledge of a particular subject
▶ fulfil your potential
▶ and contribute to something you care about – and by this means, to change it.

So, read on …

GETTING STARTED

Week 1

You may find that you walk into a well-organised and well-thought-out programme of introductions to the various aspects of life as a research student in your institution – in which case go with the flow and enjoy …

However, in our experience, the quality of introductions is highly variable. After some key introductions you may be left on your own with nothing but a handbook for company. Make sure you get a copy of this (which should be available online). As with a car manual, there's a danger you will ignore it for ages until you need it, and only *then* will you realise how valuable it is!

The most important things you can do for yourself over the first few weeks are:

▪ meet people
▪ establish a work space
▪ find your way around the department: stationery, photocopying codes, who deals with what
▪ get enrolled (identity card, library access, email)
▪ and find out when and where people meet up to socialise – and GO there!

8 What's in your handbook?

The first week anywhere new is a time of establishing yourself within the group and arranging things on your desk (if you have one). This may be tinged with frustration at bewildering administrative procedures, and perhaps anxiety about what may lie ahead. *This is the time to open the handbook and be proactive!*

The handbook will vary slightly between universities, but we guarantee it will *always* look enormous. Firstly, recognise that not all of the information is relevant to you – the book will immediately halve in size! Now recognise that, of the information that is relevant to you, only some of it is relevant to you *right now*. So, here is the key information you should look for at this stage:

▸ **A Who's Who**: a list of names of people responsible for overseeing research (e.g. the Research Students' Administrator and Chairs of various Research Committees), and other people who will be invaluable during your PhD whether you are aware of it or not – e.g. your specialist subject librarian. It is worth reading through these names so that you feel a sense of familiarity when you have to navigate the system later.

▸ **An introductory mission statement** or explanation of underlying principles.

This section defines procedures and responsibilities covering supervision, administration and assessment of research students. It will have been informed by external advisory bodies and will give you a good idea of what constitute nationally recognised standards of postgraduate education. There will also be a specific breakdown of the responsibilities of individuals and titles (e.g. Director of Studies, co-supervisors and students).

▶ **Registration**: who, where, when, and how?

▶ **Attendance and contact time requirements**, including supervisory meetings, training courses and seminars.

▶ **Progress monitoring and review**. Throughout your PhD you will have to demonstrate your academic progress, which will be assessed via a series of progress reviews or reports. Use the dates of these reports to structure the development of the project: how much time you have to write your literature review, finalise study design, obtain ethical approval and so forth.

▶ Details of **specialist services**, such as disability support, help in applying for additional funding, student representatives, complaints and appeals.

▶ **Code of good practice**: the standards expected of you and your research.

The researcher's toolkit

Your university will offer introductory courses which will develop your skills as a researcher. It is worth finding out what these are and making the effort to take any that could help you. Some universities repeat the courses during the year, so you don't have to do them all at once.

Skills you may need

These include:

- **Writing**: how to plan and structure your work, using appropriate academic English.

- **Researching**: how to use the learning resources available. Specialist librarians are often brilliant at making sure you find your way through to what you need.

- **IT skills**: training on Word and Excel may sound a bit basic, but do you know how to automatically generate a contents page? Renumber all the tables and graphs in a document with one click? Change the format of 100 references in under a minute? All this will really pay dividends. You can use them as soon as you start writing to help you structure your thesis. Consider learning to use a referencing tool like EndNote right from the start (see pp. 49–50).

- Use of **specialist programs** for your type of research: NVivo or SPSS data handling and statistical analysis packages. Knowing how you will be analysing your data is an essential prerequisite to designing the study in the first place!

- **Research methods**: these courses are generally obligatory in the first year. Consider attending one or two for subjects outside your field to expand the methods in your repertoire.

Research groups

Universities encourage their researchers to form research groups. In the sciences, these groups will be instrumental in guiding your research as you become part of the team. In other subjects, the links between researchers are less clearly stated, but it is nevertheless important to make contact and get to know the members of the group. They may offer specialised knowledge that your supervisor does not have, have useful contacts, and be great sources of information about life around the campus.

Make contact with researchers in your field in other universities: this may offer different perspectives on your work, widen your networks and give you that buzz of finding people who share your interests.

When you start, you may know exactly what you want from a PhD, the topic you are going to study, and exactly how you are going to undertake your research – but you're probably wrong.

We have yet to meet anyone who did not find a PhD to be life changing in some way. Getting started is very challenging – you have made yet another change to your identity. You are no longer solely the undergraduate, the parent, the manager, the research assistant, the musician, the teacher … you are now also a PhD student.

It can be hard to say you are a student, and it is difficult to explain what you are doing because most people have never done a PhD and few know anyone who has. People may assume you are working in 'terms' or 'semesters' and so will not realise that essentially it is a full time job, or that it comprises many nights and weekends of work when you could be relaxing. Don't worry too much about explaining: you chose to do this for yourself. Do, however, be aware that when you start it is perfectly normal to experience a period of adjustment to your 'new' life.

Supervisors know that you need extra help at the start of your PhD and should offer initial guidance and prompts to help you get going. You can help yourself by:

▶ scheduling a meeting as soon as possible

▶ being honest and asking for advice on where to start

▶ asking for another meeting after a couple of weeks – you'll have a deadline to help you focus on your initial tasks

▶ mapping out key deadlines.

Final thought

The first few days and weeks of being a PhD student may not be easy, but as you get going – reading, thinking, talking to other researchers – you will find you slip into your new identity. New issues will emerge as you become a researcher, and this is what Part 3 is about.

PhDs are training grounds for you to develop the skills you need to be a researcher. These include the ability to ask and answer questions, develop compelling arguments, write succinctly and knowledgably, debate, present talks, deal with criticism and juggle all of this with your life outside of study. Many of these skills are learnt 'on the job', and you may not realise you are learning them at the time.

This part identifies some of these key strategies so you can be proactive in hunting out opportunities to practise and eventually master them.

Establishing a relationship with your supervisor(s)

Your relationship with your supervisor(s) will be very different from your relationships with previous tutors. It is both more personal, in that you get to know each other well, and more professional, in that you will be expected to work independently and manage your working relationships. It can also be a delicate relationship, involving a shifting balance of knowledge and power. You may have one, two or even three supervisors – between us, we had this range.

The tips below will help you to use communication, organisation and diplomacy to establish a good supervisory relationship.

Getting to know each other

▶ Find out the preferred methods of communication (email/phone/face-to-face) of each of your supervisors, which may differ depending on the time of day or year.

▶ Discuss your expectations of each other early on and agree the roles and responsibilities of each member of the team. This is particularly important in multidisciplinary areas and collaborative arrangements where you may be working with supervisors representing different stakeholders in your research.

▸ Decide how often you will meet and agree meeting times and places well in advance.

Developing and managing the relationship

▸ Communicate regularly with your supervisor(s).

▸ Discuss deadlines and try to be realistic. If you cannot meet a deadline, let your supervisor(s) know promptly.

▸ Keep a record of each meeting, detailing the discussion, decisions, action points, next deadline and date of next meeting. Make copies for you and your supervisor. This record will allow you both to monitor progress and will also be essential later on when you come to filling in progress reports which require you to list the number and dates of meetings attended.

▸ Ensure that your progress is monitored regularly. This may or may not be organised in a standard way by the university/department.

▸ Where possible, organise regular joint tutorials, and copy in both/all supervisors on all email correspondence.

Assessing the changing nature of the supervisory relationship

Over the course of your PhD the balance of knowledge in your relationship with your supervisors will shift, as you become expert in your field.

▶ Be diplomatic in judging when to follow your supervisors' advice and when to assert your own argument.

Phd Start

YOUR TOPIC
YOUR SUBJECT KNOWLEDGE
YOUR RESEARCH EXPERIENCE

SUPERVISOR'S SUBJECT KNOWLEDGE

SUPERVISOR'S RESEARCH EXPERIENCE

- Your research is your own: don't be afraid to own it. If it develops in unexpected directions, be aware that your supervisors may be wary of ideas that diverge from their own areas of expertise. These, however, may be the very ideas that give your research its originality.
- If you wish to share your written work with anyone other than your supervisors, discuss this first.

Phd Finish

YOUR TOPIC
YOUR SUBJECT KNOWLEDGE
YOUR RESEARCH EXPERIENCE

SUPERVISOR'S SUBJECT KNOWLEDGE
SUPERVISOR'S RESEARCH EXPERIENCE

Managing conflict

As your research develops, conflicting opinions may arise between you and your supervisors or between your supervisors themselves. These may range from questions of bibliographic style to differing visions of the future of your project. Disagreement can be positive – a sign that you are developing your argument, a critical part of your development.

Conflict – real or apparent – does need to be acknowledged. Try to identify the problem early and address it:

▸ Organise a meeting to discuss the issue, and try to approach the problem in a business-like manner, despite your inevitable emotional investment in your own research.

▸ If your supervisors give conflicting advice, see this as a chance to discuss the different views. Disagreement is a good way to develop your argument.

If you wish to discuss changing your supervisor, approach the issue very delicately, as it may involve university politics, funding regulations, professional reputations and egos. Find out what the official procedures are and seek the advice of a member of staff independent of and/or senior to the supervisory team.

12 The ethics of research

All research activity is governed by codes of practice and/or professional codes (e.g. The British Educational Research Association). These identify three key points for consideration: general principles, the use of human and animal subjects, and intellectual property.

General principles in conducting research

These refer to your commitment to conducting research with integrity. You should be truthful in your writing and honest in your treatment of the topic and of others: you should not mislead the university or others. If you collect data, it should be open to scrutiny (in publications via peer review) and retained for examination and scrutiny (subject to issues of confidentiality).

The use of human and animal subjects

The underlying premise here is 'Treat others as you would wish to be treated'. You need to ensure that you take care of your subjects to the best of your ability at all times. You should acknowledge that difficult circumstances can arise, which need cautious and detailed ethical considerations.

Ethics committees will want to see your proposed research instruments (even if they are still in pilot form) so that they can make a judgement about your application.

Intellectual Property (IP)

All universities will have an IP policy that covers postgraduate research. In some instances special arrangements will be made – for example, if your research is funded by an external organisation where they hold the IP.

TO DO now:

▸ Get a copy of the Ethical Guidelines for your institution: read them carefully, and follow them precisely.

▸ Check with your supervisor what kind of ethical clearance (and supporting evidence) you need, especially if you will be working with people. For work with children or vulnerable adults (for example), do you need a Criminal Records Bureau (CRB) check?

▸ Work with animals also requires specific approval – check the details.

▸ How long is ethical approval likely to take from submission? It could be several months, plus slippage. Factor this into your timeline.

Tracking down and managing sources is the bread and butter of research, and a disorganised or unsystematic approach can lead to problems later on. The following points will help you to set up a coherent and manageable literature search strategy from the start.

1 Search online databases

Online databases are now the primary tool for researchers doing literature searches. They include internet search engines (e.g. Google Scholar and Google Books), library catalogues, multi-library catalogues (e.g. Copac), subject-specific databases (e.g. nineteenth-century British Library newspapers), and databases providing basic listings (e.g. Zetoc), abstracts (e.g. Index to Theses) or full texts (e.g. Ebrary, JStor and Project Muse). The range of resources can be bewildering and they change constantly, so the sooner you dive in and identify which are relevant to you, and which you can ignore, the better!

Here are some tips for using online databases. Find out:

- the online Subject Information Gateway for your research area/discipline which lists online resources (e.g. Web of Knowledge, Scirus, PubMed, Intute)
- which databases your university subscribes to and how to access them
- whether your university library runs training sessions on databases for researchers
- how the Boolean operators work – and use them. In the Boolean system (named after nineteenth-century mathematician and philosopher George Boole) the words AND, OR and NOT are combined in

different ways to produce more effective keyword searches.

Databases tend to specialise in particular types of resources. If you require a specific well-defined source (e.g. articles published in peer-reviewed scientific journals), you may only need to use a few relevant databases. However, in more interdisciplinary or creative subjects, you may need to use several databases in order to conduct a comprehensive search of the full range of resources, including books, book chapters, journals, journal articles, theses, reports, newspaper articles, museum catalogues etc.

2 Sign up for email alerts

Sign up for email alerts from publishers of books and journals in your research area, and relevant professional bodies or organisations. Keep your email alerts up to date so you will be informed of new resources in your field throughout the duration of your PhD, not just during your literature search phases. You do not want to miss the relevant book that is published just before your final submission!

3 Identify relevant archives/libraries

This can be done by:
- talking to subject librarians
- talking to researchers in your field
- using online Subject Information Gateways
- reading the 'methodology' and 'bibliography' sections of relevant scholarly books, journal articles and theses.

Once you have identified a useful archive/library, and if it is nearby, organise a visit – check what is required first. A SCONUL research card (see www.sconul.ac.uk) enables you to access a wide range of libraries for free. Find out whether you have borrowing rights, or whether you must consult resources within the library building. Alternatively, you can request an inter-library loan from your university library (check if this is limited).

4 Embrace shelf browsing

The convenience of online databases has obscured an older, perhaps more seren-dipitous method of searching for literature: shelf browsing. The grouping of books by subject in libraries and bookshops allows researchers to scan for works on similar topics, and, unlike many online databases, pick up the book and assess its useful-ness there and then. This method often throws up resources whose titles happen to omit your chosen keywords, or whose topics unexpectedly feed into yours. To shelf browse systematically, use the library catalogue (or librarian or store guide) to find the sections relating to each of your keywords (including methodological keywords), and scan each of these in turn.

5 Follow the bibliographic trail

While you may have previously regarded bibliographies as uninteresting padding at the back of books, during your literature search they acquire new value as traces of past research processes on which your project will be built. Methodology sections, footnotes and bibliographies become signposts along the trails your predecessors have trodden, allowing you to reconstruct the pathways through which existing knowledge has been constructed, and possibly discover uncharted territory. The danger in this scholarly exploration is that you can easily find yourself wandering in the wilderness far from your research aims. Keep returning to and refining your initial questions, and don't be afraid to turn back.

6 Manage your bibliography

A project the size of a PhD requires a systematic method of managing your bibliography from day one. You will quickly find that keeping references on scraps of paper becomes unmanageable. There are many possible methods of bibliography management, but two of the most common are index cards and bibliographic software.

Index cards

Advantages

▶ You can design the format of the cards and include as many fields of information as you wish.

▶ Can be updated anywhere (e.g. in the library), as long as you take your cards with you (but not all of them!).

▶ Not affected by computer failure.

Disadvantages

▶ Depending on your ordering system, may be more difficult to search by subject or other variables.

▶ May be cumbersome to carry around, particularly if large.

Bibliographic software

University libraries usually support a particular bibliographic software package (like EndNote or RefWorks), but there are many free packages available.

Advantages

- Can be searched by any variable, e.g. subject, keywords.
- Can hold large numbers of references without becoming cumbersome to carry.
- Allows easy referencing while writing as citations may be inserted directly from the bibliographic software, allowing automatic generation of a bibliography and automatic update of styles.
- Some software packages allow bibliographies to be shared amongst researchers.

Disadvantages

- Can only be updated by computer.
- Vulnerable to computer failure – always back up! Work out your back-up system, using a memory (USB) stick, CD, various locations – but at the very least turn on the 'autosave' function to save your work every half hour, especially when you are working on data.

Use your chapters as a filing system

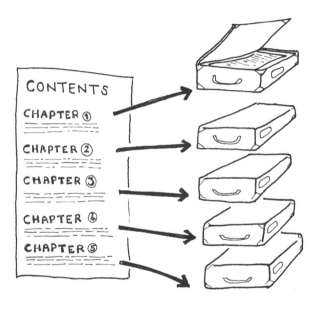

Ahh ... where did I find that diagram ...?

Whatever system you use to keep track of your sources, make sure you have one! Research students have to be meticulous in their care to credit the work of others – as they would wish their research to be credited.

It is easy to lose track of where this or that came from. Issues of attribution and copyright will become even more important in future as all PhD theses become available electronically.

How you read is just as important as *what* and *how much* you read. Try reading each source from the following perspectives:

Learning from the source

▶ Which methodology is used?
▶ What is the overall argument?
▶ How is the argument constructed?

Critical analysis of the source

▶ Who is the author? What is her/his perspective?
▶ Which readership does the source address?
▶ Why has it been written?
▶ When was it written?
▶ Is the methodology suited to the research aim?
▶ Is the argument based upon any assumptions?
▶ Are the conclusions logically drawn from the argument?

Making connections to other texts
- Which other authors are cited in the source?
- What is its relationship to the development of theory in the field?
- What are the similarities and differences between this argument and others on the same topic?
- What is its contribution to research in the field?

*What does the source **not** say?*
- Are there any gaps in the argument?
- Does the author indicate any areas that require further research?
- How could this question have been approached differently?
- How could this methodology be applied to different subjects?

Making connections to your research
- What are the similarities and differences between the aims of this research and your own?
- Do you agree with the argument presented? If not, why not?
- Might the source influence your methodology?
- Does the source provide any relevant examples that could support your argument?
- Does the source point towards interesting theoretical perspectives?
- What questions are raised that may require future research?

Note making tips

▶ Summarise articles as you go: What's useful in this article to me? What do I come back for? How is it relevant to my research?

▶ Keep your ideas distinct from those of the author in your notes, either by using a separate column or a different coloured pen.

▶ Make sure it is clear which sections of your notes are direct quotations.

▶ Record full bibliographic details of each source you use.

▶ Record page numbers, ensuring it is clear which notes were taken from which page.

▶ And avoid getting drawn into irrelevant side issues – however fascinating!

You are not expected to know everything, but you do need to know where to go to find out more.

Being a researcher in a multi- or interdisciplinary area

You may become engaged in inter- or multidisciplinary research because your research question requires a number of disciplinary perspectives, or your PhD may be part of a wider, funded research project staffed by researchers from a range of disciplines. In either case, it is worth understanding the peculiarities of this type of research, as it can involve some distinctive opportunities and challenges.

First, some definitions:

Multidisciplinary research: Research in which a central question is approached from a number of disciplinary perspectives, without attempting to integrate or reconcile them. It is usually conducted by teams composed of researchers from different disciplines.

Interdisciplinary research: Research into areas beyond or crossing traditional disciplinary boundaries, and which therefore requires the integration of knowledge or methodologies from different disciplines. It can be carried out by a single researcher or a team. Some interdisciplinary areas are already reasonably well defined, such as biochemistry and cybernetics, while others are uncharted.

Many of the newer academic disciplines, such as cultural studies and dance studies, are inherently interdisciplinary, because they focus on questions or objects of study that are not encompassed by the traditional disciplines. In the absence of established methodologies, they tend to draw on a range of disciplinary perspectives in their analyses.

Opportunities of inter- and multidisciplinary research

This type of research allows you to:

▶ address questions beyond the scope of a single discipline, e.g. climate change

▶ question the assumptions underlying a particular disciplinary approach or methodology

▶ find new areas of research, and make an easily identifiable contribution to existing knowledge

▶ apply your existing disciplinary knowledge in an innovative way.

Challenges and demands of inter- and multidisciplinary research

Abandoning the safety of your disciplinary home and exploring the uncharted territory between disciplines can be difficult and isolating, leaving you open to attack from established disciplinary fortresses. The following will help you to meet these challenges.

▶ Researching beyond tried and tested disciplinary methods requires resourcefulness, creativity and determination.

▶ Understanding the premises of an unfamiliar discipline requires you to question your own assumptions and take on a different worldview.

- Finding a common ground between different disciplinary ideologies and languages requires commitment to understanding each discipline in its own right, and the time and attention to detail to find a credible synthesis.

- Managing discipline-specific supervisors (especially if your supervisory team encompasses several disciplines) requires sensitivity, the ability to enthuse your supervisors with your idea, and the strength of purpose to avoid getting side-tracked down a more disciplinary path.

- Publishing interdisciplinary work requires research into appropriate journals and editors, and perhaps an openness towards alternative methods of publishing, such as online journals.

16 Writing up or writing down?

There are many different ways of using writing in your research, and you don't need to wait until you have a fully formed argument before you start. Here are some writing strategies that you can begin using straight away:

An introductory narrative: the 'story' of your research. How and why did I come up with the idea and where might it lead?
Using it: as part of your proposal, and/or your introduction? It helps your reader get a sense of your commitment and interest.

Survey pieces: initial forays into the field. What's out there?
Using it: with a bit of luck you will be able to use these in your proposal.

Beyond summary: do the reading and come back with an overview in which you start to draw out the argument you are beginning to see.
Using it: the basis of your literature review?

Write to understand, not to explain: your ideas always develop as you form the words on the page, so use writing as a way to hone thoughts and make connections, without worrying that it needs to be part of the final thesis.

Using it: much of this writing will not make it into the thesis, but will allow you to write as if you are already an expert.

Write blocs of ideas: and see where they fit.
Using it: hopefully it will fit somewhere later. It could be costly in energy, but might be good to get you going.

A journal, log or blog: so nothing is lost or duplicated – with you at all times for ideas, jottings, sources, contacts, record of developing thought and research progress.
Using it: for discussions with your supervisor, acknowledgements, material for early drafts.

Final thought

When you have begun to think about or experience the issues outlined in this section, you have made the transition to becoming a researcher. You are ready to do some hard thinking and planning as you move towards your first major milestone – your research proposal.

Part 4 invites you to join the WORKSHOP, pick up a pencil and start mapping your onward journey.

THE WORKSHOP –
Mapping your research process

This section is different from the rest of the guide. Here we invite you to do some practical work – to join our 'workshop'. The purpose is to help you clarify your thinking and sharpen your research question in preparation for writing about your research plans in the early stages of your research (see Part 5). You do not have to do it all at once, but do take it in sequence. Start when you have a clear 15 minutes to do the first workshop activity, and go from there.

To write about your planned research you have to look ahead, to peer into the next few years and imagine what you will be doing at any given time. This makes it a challenging task: here you are, right at the beginning of your research, uncertain about what lies ahead, yet having to think through all the stages of the next few years and set it out as a 'plan'.

This, of course, is precisely why you have to do it. Not only does your institution need to have a concrete plan of your research, and know that you know what you are planning to do – but so do you.

Mapping your journey

Your research plan – like any outline – can provide you with a useful point of reference throughout the journey that lies before you. So it's worth investing time and effort in trying to envisage the journey ahead as clearly as possible.

Workshop 1: The road ahead

Try to visualise your pathway from where you are *now* (don't look back and include what you've done up to now), to when you complete your doctorate, way off in the future.

→ Take a large sheet of paper – A3 is ideal
→ Put yourself at the bottom: **start**
→ Show your completion point at the top: **finish**
→ Sketch the journey in between
→ Mark in the phases
→ Show trouble spots and milestones
→ Mark out the time phases

Give yourself 15 minutes.

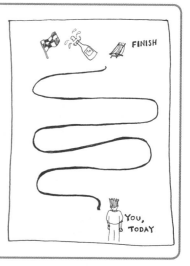

Here are some maps sketched by PhD students at the beginning of their PhD, and their commentaries.

Two journeys

Ally's map

Looking back, this early map looks just like my PhD – it progressed in cycles. I was constantly feeding in information and it was cyclical because that worked with how I worked. I didn't work on it consistently despite being 'full time'. Sometimes I felt like writing and did a lot and at other times, I would not work on it for some weeks, or even months.

Central to the process was talking about it as I went along: that was crucial to the development of my ideas.

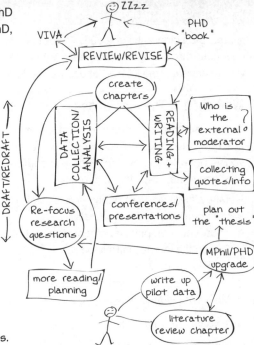

Reproduced with thanks to Dr Alison Daubney

Simon's map

I'm doing my PhD by publication – it's about the role of mental toughness (MT) in the performance of elite athletes. There are three studies on different aspects, and each of these will become a publication:

- what MT is
- how it operates
- how it manifests itself.

Then there will be a fourth publication – off the top of the page. This will be about the potential of my findings about mental toughness to guide interventions with athletes. But until I know exactly what it is, I can't see how to do it. That's my project ...

Reproduced with thanks to Simon Crampton (1st year PhD student)

Why do this map?

▶ This scribbly sketch – a 'rich picture' – can make the PhD seem more do-able and real and many people work better with visual images.

▶ It helps you do the groundwork for your research plan, thinking about the research process and timescales.

▶ It makes you think about key points like publication and conference possibilities from the start.

▶ It keeps your eye on the ball – it's there to refer back to, keeping yourself on track.

▶ It gives you something to discuss with your supervisor: they can see the what/where/how as you do, and might be able to spot the pitfalls …

What is your question? What are you trying to find out?

You have, of course, already done quite a bit of thinking about your topic. You have already been accepted by your institution on the basis of the statement of research interest you submitted as part of your application. You may have done a Master's related to the topic and you have been reading around it since you started. You already know quite a bit about it.

Now you are getting started on your PhD proper it is a little different. You need to move from having identified a research topic area to pinpointing an aim that will take you to the gap in current knowledge you are curious about. This is where you will be generating new knowledge and making your contribution to research in the field.

Your research aim is arguably the single most important driver for your PhD. It will form the basis of your research question, focus your literature search, shape your research design and determine your methods. In short, it will inform your research activity over the next few years. It will also constantly evolve and refocus and you will revisit it frequently.

Supervisors know this. They know that what matters is that at any given moment your aim reflects what you are really trying to find out and achieve, so your activity is purposeful, researchable and focused. They will work with you as it evolves.

It is worth investing good thinking time in doing the groundwork that will enable you to identify and articulate an aim that:

▶ reflects your core question (not a side issue or preliminary inquiry)
▶ is not too general – a 'review' activity
▶ is not too specific or incapable of sustaining research at PhD level
▶ is clean, lean and doesn't have sub-questions (objectives), side issues or bits of methodology dangling off it.

Here are some thinking activities to help you work this through.

Workshop 2: A brainstorm

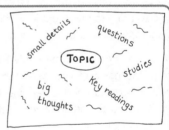

→ Take a large sheet of paper – A3 again.
→ In the centre draw a circle. In it write your research topic with only as much detail as you are confident about right now. If that is quite general, put that down. If you are quite specific in your focus, write that.
→ *Fill* the rest of the sheet with everything that pours out of your mind in any order ... anything and everything. Don't worry about connecting them – that can follow.
→ Just go for it – take 5 minutes.

Now talk about it. Use your mind map as a prompt to talk to someone – anyone – about your plans for your research. If you can't find anyone, explain it to a pot plant, the cat, a chair … What matters is that you talk about it, and hear yourself talking about it. 2 minutes.

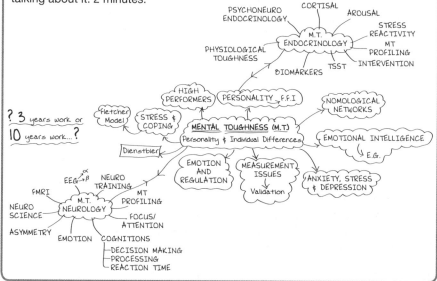

Workshop 3: <u>What</u> <u>exactly</u> are you <u>trying</u> to <u>find out</u>?

Read this question out loud with the emphasis on the underlined words.

Now answer it as simply and as clearly as you can:

→ Start: *'I'm trying to find out …'* and finish the sentence. No more.

→ Write it down, in plain language so that someone not in your field could understand the nature of your inquiry (use technical terms only where essential).

> I'm trying to find out …
>
> ....
>
> ....
>
> ....

→ You may just have written down your research question. Test it out:
  ▶ Is it clear to you?
  ▶ Is it a single sentence, without lots of subclauses?
  ▶ Does it point you to two, three, maybe four different areas of literature?
  ▶ Does it have a single focus?

→ Reconsider your question if:

  ▶ it has been around for a while: is it the same as the question you presented in your application? This could mean you are very focused – or that you haven't moved on in the past months.

  ▶ it has lots of bits to it. Some of these may be sub-questions which you can include as objectives, but need to take out of your main research question.

  ▶ you already know the answer. You won't be researching or finding out, but seeking to justify.

  ▶ it has two (or three) parts – one of these is likely to be the eventual goal, the others, research objectives on the way there.

  ▶ you are not happy with it. You are the best judge of whether your question matches you and what you really want to do.

There are no rights or wrongs to the question you want to ask. It is in the nature of research that no one will have asked *your* question before. In the unlikely event that they have, you will soon find out about it, and use their findings as a spring-board for refocusing your question. So let's not worry about this.

Instead, try a few mental gymnastics and see if they help you move towards a research question you are happy with.

Workshop 4: Look at the little words

I'm trying to find out …

… the ways in which (this) shows itself in (that)

… about the association between (this) and (that) in …

… what (this) tells us about (that)

… the effect(s)/impact of (this) on (that).

It can be tempting to shorten this formulation to 'How …?' but the fuller articulation may help you see the many strands of your inquiry.

Some questions directly reflect a researcher's drive towards their research question:

Each of these bullets will be substantial research areas.

I'm trying to find out
… if …
… whether …

On the face of it, this formula suggests a yes/no answer – either it does or it doesn't. This is probably not what you intend, so try recognising this complexity in your wording:
… the extent to which … *or* to what extent …?
… How central/effective …?

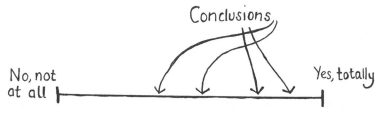

This will help you think about where your inquiry might lead. Different strands/factors/causes/elements might find a different resting point on the scale, between 'no, not at all' and 'yes, totally'. None is likely to end up at the extremes.

Why are you researching this question?

This is the billion dollar question – the one everyone wants to ask, but may be too polite to articulate! The answers you give to this question are fundamental to your research. You probably have several reasons, and in them will lie the rationale for your research, the justification that will inform your argument from start to finish.

Workshop 5: *Why* are you researching this?

The question can be answered at several levels. At the very least you will probably have

▶ a personal reason
▶ an academic reason.

Only you need to acknowledge your personal reason(s). Nevertheless it is important, even if you never mention it to anyone – and there is no reason why you should. It is what will drive you on, and ultimately it is where you will derive your satisfaction.

So ... between you and your piece of paper, *why* are you doing this?

What is your PERSONAL reason?

My PERSONAL reason:

....

....

....

Here are some of the PERSONAL reasons PhD students have noted:

Because …

    … I want to explore … / why …

    … I've noticed that … and wondered whether …

    … I want to feed this back into professional training

    … I don't think (…) works

    … I've always been fascinated by … and I want to find out …

    … I want to change (…) / make a difference … to …

    … it's a passion …

And what is your ACADEMIC reason?

My ACADEMIC reason:

....

....

....

....

....

ACADEMIC reasons PhD students have given include:

... *little research on ... from the perspective of ...*

... *add a valuable insight into ... / increase understanding of ...*

... *the literature in this area focuses on ... not ...*

... *gain a better understanding of the process of ...*

... *to challenge the notions of ...*

... *to bridge the gap between (...) and (...)*

... *it's a new phenomenon, and there is little research ...*

The academic reasons will articulate the gap in knowledge … of course! Once you have identified a gap in the knowledge in an area you want to research, you are very close to your research question, and to taking the first steps towards filling that gap.

These academic reasons provide the 'justification' or 'rationale' for your research that you need to set out in your proposal.

Now check:

→ Who, in the wider academic community, will be interested in it?
→ Does it contribute to a current stream of developing research interest?
→ What might the impact of your research be? For whom?

If you have done Workshops 1–5 in one sitting, it's time now to take a break!

You've done some hard thinking – now stand back and see how it all feels. See how it fits with what you know is out there: the literature, the norms, practices, methodologies and theoretical models current in your research field. The workshops in this section are designed to focus on this.

Workshop 6: Find your research comfort zone

Research moves between the well-established, emerging evidence and perspectives, and the unanswered questions. Where is your question in all this?

→ Try moving your question up and down the comfort zone – getting more general (to allow you to refocus and connect with the major literature) and more specific (to find your question), till you feel you have got it right.

→ Now check: is it achievable within the timescale?

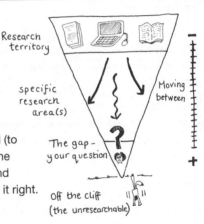

Research territory

specific research area(s)

Moving between

The gap – your question

Off the cliff (the unresearchable)

Workshop 7: Sit your research interest within different theoretical models

A theoretical model comprises a set of assumptions about a concept or system. There will be a number of models around in your discipline – what are they? And how might they shape your research question, and your research design?

Sit your question within different theoretical models …

… and see how your perspective changes.

How will you do it?

This question takes you to your approach, your methodology, and the methods you plan to use. This is highly discipline specific, as these comments from PhD students indicate:

- '... the process of research consists of a continuous alternation between reading and writing ... The methodology drew on history, anthropology, and cultural studies.'
- 'I decided upon a mixed-method approach. This was considered highly contentious ...'
- '... the project gradually transformed to include quantitative and qualitative work.'
- 'I enjoy the process of hypothesis-driven research. The constant refining and testing of hypotheses, getting ever closer to an answer, and trying to explain unexpected results and rethink my approach, is really rewarding.'

These comments were made by people who can now put 'Doctor' before their name! In retrospect, statements like this can make devising your methodology sound easy. It rarely is. Whether at the overall level of 'research design' or 'approach' or the specific level of 'methods', the question of *how* you carry out your research is complex and it is the outcome of reading, pondering, tweaking, imagining, revising, rethinking ... and so on.

The key thing is that the methods you adopt must be consistent with your aim. If your aim evolves, so must your methods. If you decide to adopt different methods, you need to revisit your aim – and always be prepared to justify your decisions.

What is your argument?

A good clear aim drives the whole research process, including the writing. When you have a direction it helps you to see your 'argument', your line of reasoning, supported by the evidence of your research. In your final thesis, this will run from start to finish, and become the 'golden thread of argument' that gives your thesis its cohesion, its purpose and ultimately its value.

At the point of writing your proposal, you won't have the argument of your eventual thesis (see Simon's comments, p. 67) but you will need to make the case for researching the question. You want your reader to think, 'Ah yes, I can see the argument for researching this. I can see that there is a gap here; it will make a contribution to the literature by following the path set out here.'

RESEARCH QUESTION

CONCLUSIONS & IMPLICATIONS

The golden thread of argument

As a research student you are aiming to fill a gap in knowledge or understanding of some phenomenon. Think of this as 'making a contribution' to the literature on the subject. It is less pressurising, more respectful of research in your field and more constructive than trying to achieve 'originality'.

Your research will build on research that has gone before: 'standing on the shoulders of giants' is how it is often described. If you did set out with a direction of inquiry that is totally at odds with traditions of thinking within your discipline(s), you would be in a lonely place and supervisors would find it difficult to supervise you. Rather, if you think of it as putting a little piece of the jigsaw in place – a jump-off point for the questions of the next researcher – you can see how you can make a 'contribution' to the ongoing debates in the discipline and, via this route, to knowledge.

Your 'originality' may lie in your material, in your approach, in your findings, interpretation, analysis and (always) in your writing.

Small steps, big contribution

One PhD researcher's aim was to find out more about the biodiversity of coniferous plantations. She found a study that demonstrated that the biodiversity in the outer 50 metres of a plantation was impoverished. This helped her to hone her research question – to find out how biodiverse the next tranche of woodland is. So she focused her study on the next 100 metres in.

Fascinating! This (oversimplified) sketch illustrates a number of points about the nature of the 'contribution':

Outer 50m: biodiversity reduced

Next 100m: Question – Is biodiversity reduced? How far?

... and what are the implications for woodland management?

Based on Dr Imogen Palmer's contribution to a workshop, with thanks.

▸ **Small steps, big implications:**
If the biodiversity of the outer 150 metres of a plantation is impoverished, narrow strips of plantation offer a reduced habitat to wildlife. This is high-impact research – potentially of immense importance to forestry and wildlife protection agencies.

▸ **Future researchers** in related disciplines can use this research as a springboard for theirs. It opens up the next wave of questions: which species do/don't thrive in these outer 'bands' of plantations? How far do you have to go into the plantation to find 'full' biodiversity (and what is this?)? The jigsaw of knowledge expands …

Workshop 8: What is your contribution?

Jot down answers to these questions:

→ How will your research contribute to knowledge in the area?
→ How will it contribute to understanding?
→ What might the implications of your research be?
→ Who might be interested in your contribution?
→ Why and how might it be used? How might the impact of this research ripple outwards?

You will be able to draw on this in the conclusion of your proposal, and eventually, in a changed form, in your thesis.

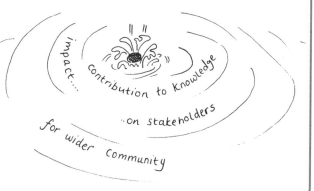

Final thought

Part 4 should have felt like hard work. You will draw on the thinking you have done there many times as you plan your research.

Part 5 is about these pieces of writing.

PART

5 WRITING RESEARCH PLANS

At several points in the first year of a PhD you will be asked to capture the thinking you explored in The Workshop (Part 4) in various pieces of writing. We use the term 'research plan' in this part to describe several pieces of writing you are likely to be asked to do.

Any research plan you write will, in effect, offer your reader answers to these key project planning questions:*

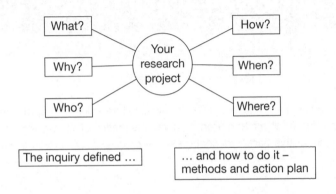

Of these six questions, the most important is 'Why?' This will become the justification which runs through your research from start to finish. This is the question that will be foremost in your reader's mind.

*Referred to as 'strategic questions' in *Getting critical* in this series.

Your readers will be looking to see:

▶ *your clarity of purpose*: What is your aim? What are you trying to find out? What kind of answer are you looking for?

▶ *your awareness of the scope* of the relevant literature – and gaps within it

▶ *your justification or rationale* for your research

▶ *your research methodology* comprising the design and methods you plan to use, looking at soundness, appropriateness and feasibility

▶ *the relevance and significance* (not the same thing …) to the field

▶ and *your strategy* for managing the project, including your timescales.

In short, your readers will be looking both for the essential qualities of research that is likely to make a contribution to the field, and for evidence that you can manage this ambitious project.

Your task is to make sure your reader can see these qualities in your writing.

Workshop 9: Forward planning

What will you have to write in the initial period of your research? You are likely to be asked to produce both short and longer pieces of writing for different purposes at various points. Check this table against your handbook.

	Title and purpose(s)	Date (approx)
Short piece(s) (1500–2000 words) This might be described as: • Registration • Progress review(s) • Critical review(s) • Other?	1 2 3	1 2 3
A longer piece (4000–6000 words) This might be described as: • 'Upgrade' or 'transfer document' (from MPhil to PhD) • Formal proposal • Other?		

The elements

The exact format of these plans will vary between institutions, disciplines and departments with varying details in the sections. Compare the list of possible elements on the next page with what you are asked to produce.

The shaded sections are considered in Chapters 19 and 20. These are the two key areas you will always have to write: an introduction and a literature review, however long or short the piece is.

	Short	Longer
Title … or working title that fits what you are planning now.		
Introduction The field of study, why it is important and the steps that led you to your particular research question.		
Literature review A critical discussion of what others have done, showing you are aware of the issues and debates in your field. It will show how your proposed research relates (in content and/or methods) to other work in the field.		
Aim and objectives Your main research question (or hypothesis, problem or proposition), and sub-questions (objectives).		
Research design/methodology/ methods The 'here's how I'm going to tackle it': theories that will inform your approach; specific methods you will employ and why. Expected outcomes.		
Ethical issues or approval		

	Short	Longer
Chapter plan		
Training, facilities and resources Available and required.		
Work plan and timetable to completion Show possible publication/conference paper points		
Indicative bibliography Not an exhaustive listing of everything you have read, but a representative sample.		

What is a literature review?

A literature review is a **summary**, **synthesis** and **evaluation** of the available literature on a particular topic. It is a process, not necessarily a chapter title. You may have several chapters, suitably titled, that deal with different aspects of the relevant literature. Your reading from Day 1 will contribute to it.

A good literature review will:
- identify a discrete research area (in interdisciplinary studies this may include several previously separate areas)
- provide a summary of the research area, pointing out trends, shifts and connections
- organise and interpret the material in response to a particular research question
- highlight contentious, well-researched and under-researched topics
- critically evaluate the literature
- position your own research in relation to the area you have studied
- probably form the first chapter of your thesis.

Get started on this as early as possible.

Writing a literature review for your research plan or proposal

The literature review you write for your proposal will form the basis for the one you will eventually write for your thesis. It needs to:

▶ provide a rationale for your research proposal
▶ identify your field of research and position your proposal within it
▶ show an awareness of the boundaries of your research
▶ demonstrate that you can critically analyse, synthesise and structure material
▶ indicate the future direction of your project, based on an initial summary of the existing literature.

Why do a literature review?

The literature review is an essential part of the PhD proposal and thesis. This is because it is an important part of the research process, which allows you to:

▶ gain an overview of the area in which you will be working
▶ identify the gap in existing research that your project will address
▶ avoid duplicating previous research
▶ learn from others' mistakes
▶ build on existing knowledge
▶ define the boundaries of your research

- assess existing methodologies and concepts
- construct an informed rationale for your research.

Structuring your literature review

Literature searches often uncover a range of sources from different periods, disciplines and perspectives. This diversity can make structuring your literature review a challenge. If you are a visual thinker, the following strategies may help:

Draw a map of the different research areas covered by your literature review, paying attention to the relationships between the areas. Where would you position your own research on this map?

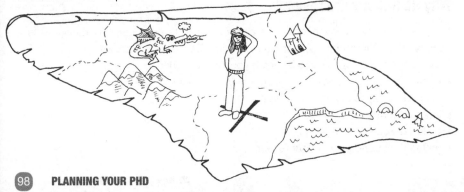

Draw a tree of the research developments in your research area, paying attention to how each branch connects with the earlier ones. Where does your research fit?

Here are some possible ways of structuring your literature review:

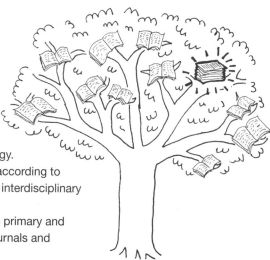

- *Chronologically*: according to the order in which research was produced.
- *Thematically*: grouping historically disparate sources according to theme.
- *Methodologically*: grouping sources according to methodology.
- *By discipline*: grouping sources according to discipline – this may be useful in interdisciplinary studies.
- *By type of source*: e.g. subdivide primary and secondary sources, or books, journals and newspapers.
- *By your use of the source*: e.g. subdivide sources relevant to your subject matter from sources relevant to your methodology.

The purpose of any introduction is to draw your reader into your argument and lead them to your aim(s) – not to offer them a tour of your subject area. Once you see this clearly, you will focus on looking out to your reader, not looking in to your knowledge. You can then see your introduction as a series of 'moves'.

And of course, you write your introduction *last* (you can't take your reader on a journey until you know where you are going). You set out the process that took you to your research question (or aim) step by step. The logic of this reasoning and the way you articulate it becomes your argument.

You will find yourself writing a version of your introduction many times, at different points in your research. The introduction to each version of your research plan takes your reader to your question – the 'door' to your eventual inquiry. There is a whole new journey beyond this. You want your reader to be saying at this point: *'Yeah! Go for it! I quite see why you need to research this, and I really want to see what you find out ...'*

The 'moves' of an introduction

So how do you do it? The introduction below illustrates this movement, the flow of argument that brings the reader to the writer's aim.

Attitudes of physiotherapists in Botswana to treating people living with HIV/AIDS

Kambole and Struthers (2009)

What's in your reader's mind before they start to read? Not much? It's your space, your argument. Make it!

Move 1: The context/issue/ problem	Your reader's instinct will be to just note the topic. You, however, want to engage them in your argument from the first line. To do this you might:
The Human Immunodeficiency Virus (HIV) and Acquired Immune Deficiency Syndrome (AIDS) have continued to spread in Southern Africa despite public awareness campaigns related to prevention. By the end of 2005, Botswana had a national HIV prevalence of 24% among adults in a population of only 1,640,115 (UNAIDS 2006). Although there are reduced global infection rates, Botswana remains one of the hardest stricken countries in the world (UNAIDS 2007).	• start with a bald statement of the issue: 'This is what it's about ...' • locate it in context (geographic, thematic, historic) • include a key figure to illustrate the scale of the issue • engage the reader's attention with an arresting thought. *And before your reader has the chance to ask 'Why are you engaged in this?' you move swiftly to Move 2*

Move 2: The research territory	You want to show how your highly specific research sits within the bigger picture – the 'what is known' in the field. To do this you are likely to:
While many people living with HIV/AIDS (PLWHA) on anti-retroviral drugs (ARVs) are experiencing an improved life span (Palella et al. 1998), they are also experiencing more chronic health problems (Wood et al. 2000) and impairment and disability is increasing (Rusch et al. 2003).	<ul><li>indicate the importance of the whole research field, and define it</li><li>identify key research within it – this is likely to be the most heavily referenced section of your introduction.</li></ul>
	'Hmm … OK there's important work in this field …' thinks your reader. And before they can think 'Where are YOU going?' you're answering their unasked question …
Move 3: Specific research area	You are now within your topic area, your niche, identifying specific research that your work relates to. Your focus narrows. Here you might:
As a consequence, physiotherapists are working with increasing numbers of people with HIV related conditions (Gale 2003). Studies have reported on the beneficial role of physiotherapy in the management of neurological, musculoskeletal, respiratory, and painful syndromes among HIV infected people (Gale 2003; Jose and Balan 2002; Ondonga 2002; Sacky 1998).	<ul><li>indicate related studies, showing how they differ from your research area</li><li>highlight assumptions in previous research</li><li>question or critique the methods or approach of previous research</li><li>or show how these methods are appropriate for a different line of inquiry from yours.</li></ul>
	'I can see where you're going …' thinks your reader – who is now sitting up, waiting to see what you will do about this.

Move 4: The gap in previous research	You move in and occupy the space you have identified in previous research. You give your justification or rationale for your research. You may show that:
However, there are limited studies on attitudes of physiotherapists towards treating people living with HIV/AIDS (Voors 2000), despite research done on the attitudes of other healthcare professionals (Worthington et al. 2005).	• more knowledge is needed in order to … • previous research doesn't show xyz • you can justify your question because there is a gap in knowledge which it is worthwhile to fill in order to …
	Your reader has totally grasped your argument now. You have made your case for your research. They are excited about reading on … Just one thing …
Move 5: Your aim	Make a short, clear statement about the central aim or purpose of your research (the outcome of your thinking in The Workshop, Part 4). 'In this study I aim to …'
The aim of this study was to determine the attitudes of physiotherapists in Gaborone and Ramotswa, Botswana, towards treating people living with HIV/AIDS.	
	Home and dry! You have a satisfied reader, with a clear overview of your purpose and argument.
	Details about the aim and the objectives that feed into it will come later.

Source: Kambole and Struthers (2009) reproduced with the kind permission of the publishers.

This is a wonderfully short introduction. It does, however, have the structure, the 'moves' of any introduction, long or short. Try it!

Workshop 10: Your introduction in five moves

Try writing the topic sentence for each move of your introduction. You might like to start with Move 5, the aim.

You can then develop each move into a couple of sentences (for a very short introduction as in the example above), a couple of paragraphs, or even short sections … depending on what you are writing.

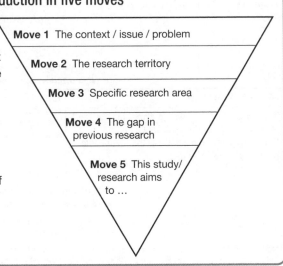

Move 1 The context / issue / problem

Move 2 The research territory

Move 3 Specific research area

Move 4 The gap in previous research

Move 5 This study/ research aims to …

A reality check

Do a careful analysis of introductions in your discipline:

▶ three or four peer-reviewed articles

▶ a Master's dissertation

▶ a PhD

▶ and, if possible (which it may not be) a research plan or proposal.

Compare the structure of each with the outline above and with each other. They will have some similarities (your task is to identify these) and certainly some differences, reflecting the norms in your discipline or the length of the piece. Articles are perhaps the most useful models as they tend to be short and they set out the thinking – the argument – most succinctly.

It is an artifice, isn't it?

You will be struck by how any introduction is a carefully crafted artifice. As a reader you encounter it first. As a writer you write it last when you know the journey ahead. Over to you to construct yours – when you have written the rest!

Final thought

This isn't the end of planning! Part 6 invites you to look ahead to see your entire research journey (Part 4, Workshop 1), and to plan when and how you will share your research findings with your research community and other potential users of your research.

PLANNING YOUR PHD

FINDING AUDIENCES FOR YOUR RESEARCH

As you start your PhD, the prospect of disseminating your well-considered ideas to the world may seem distant and daunting. Alternatively, you may feel driven by your desire to make a difference to the situation or problem that prompted your research. Either way, sharing and publishing your research during your PhD is a must: it is the means by which you bring your research to the attention of others who have an interest in the field, and to external stakeholders who may be the eventual users of your research.

Sharing your work will also have a positive impact both on the PhD itself and on your post-doctoral career. So start planning now, so that by the time you complete you have a track record of conference contributions and publication.

Attending and giving papers at conferences allows you to:

- gain access to the latest research
- network with researchers in your field and identify potential external examiners and future collaborators
- feel part of a research community
- hone your ideas into a presentable form
- receive feedback on your research
- practise presentation skills for your MPhil/PhD upgrade or future lecturing career.

It is a good idea to attend at least one conference before you give your first conference paper.

The process

1 Sign up to generic and subject-specific conference email alerts in order to receive Calls For Papers. You may also receive these via subject email lists or helpful colleagues or find them on subject-specific websites.

2 When you receive a Call For Papers relevant to your research, you may want to discuss the possibility of either attending the conference or submitting a proposal with your supervisor.

3 Submit a proposal by the deadline, usually in the form of an abstract, and other information about the requirements of your presentation.

4 If your proposal is accepted, write the paper in time to ask for feedback from your supervisors. Give a departmental presentation for practice.

5 Book travel and accommodation for the conference. You may be able to apply for some funding for this from your university.

6 Remember to register for the conference (register early to get the 'early bird' rate) and pay the conference fee (again, your university may offer funding). This is usually necessary even if you are giving a paper.

7 Practise the presentation, especially the coordination of speech with slides if you are using them.

8 Deliver the presentation and answer any questions from the audience.
9 Talk afterwards to interested members of the audience – this is a good opportunity for networking.

It is a good idea to ask someone in the audience in advance to note the questions and your responses. The questions are one of the most important aspects of giving a conference talk. They could point you to a question for your viva, to further research, to what people find interesting or problematic.

Many conferences offer publication of your paper in the conference proceedings. This can be a good step towards the next stage in disseminating your research: publication.

Why publish?

For people who are taking the PhD by publication route, publishing is the core business, but for those who are producing a 'big book' PhD, publication along the way is equally important for a number of reasons, such as to:

▶ develop your ideas, arguments and writing
▶ give you tangible milestones in the PhD process
▶ gain feedback from peer reviewers, bringing in different or unexpected perspectives
▶ learn about the differences between writing a thesis and writing a journal article
▶ stake a claim to your research area, and to your intellectual property
▶ gain experience in defending your work – useful for the viva
▶ build up a publication record, necessary for gaining an academic job after your PhD.

Publication will increase your value to your own and other institutions by building up possible submissions to research monitoring processes, in particular the Research

Excellence Framework (REF). Once your work is published, it can be cited by others. In REF terms, work becomes more 'valuable' the more it is cited.

Publication also allows you to frame your research for different audiences or for a particular audience who may not read your thesis, and so it expands the range of eventual users of your research. It is also the means by which your research can have an effect on ideas, policies, actions or future research, the 'impact' that the REF will be looking for.

Developing a publication strategy

You may have considered your publication strategy in your initial time plan for your research (see p. 93). You might want to consider publishing at the following stages of the research process:

→ After your **literature review**

Have you developed an original synthesis of the existing literature? Or identified an interesting trend, pattern or gap in the literature? Don't underestimate the publication potential of this early stage of your research as reviews get good citation rates.

→ After formulating and testing your **methodology**

Do you have something innovative to say about existing approaches and models, or your approach?

→ When you have some outcomes from a **phase** of your research

→ When you have identified the **conclusions** of your project

What are the implications of your findings? How do they relate to the existing literature? Do they indicate the way forward for future research?

Hints for publication

Not all of the hints below will be relevant to you, and you may disagree with some, but you may find a couple of points you can use in planning your own approach to publication.

Hint 1: Get familiar with the journals
Which journals are well respected in your field? Which are peer-reviewed? Publication in peer-reviewed journals is a marker of esteem, and also ensures that you will get useful, critical feedback. Are any of your colleagues on journal editorial boards? Approach them – for *advice* (of course!)
Hint 2: Think ahead
The publication process usually takes at least 9 months from submission. Incorporate this delay into your strategy.

Hint 3: Find out the authorship conventions for doctoral students in your discipline

Is authorship attributed to the PhD student alone or both student and supervisor? If the latter, approach your supervisor about finding a problem you can work on together. This can be a potential win/win situation: your supervisor won't have the time, so you do the research; you don't have their networks or craft of writing, so you learn.

Hint 4: Match your paper to the models in the journal you are submitting to

Scrutinise the format, style, referencing and instructions to authors.

Hint 5: Draft and redraft

Your first draft will not be good enough.
Draft 2 will be better. You will have matched it to the model.
Draft 3 will be better still. You'll have worked on your language and expression. Show it to some colleagues and ask for their comments.
Draft 4 should be looking good … ready to submit?
Each redraft makes it a more sophisticated product, and you learn the craft of writing.

Hint 6: Ask the editor for _advice_

At Draft 3 or 4 (when you have acted on feedback), send it to the editor _not_ as a submission but to ask 'Do you have any advice?'

Hint 7: Don't pick a fight

Academic debates in any field tend to be polarised. Don't pick a side, but show the thread you are pursuing. Use moderate and reasoned language. In a peer-reviewed journal your paper will be sent to specialists in precisely your field.

Hint 8: Rejection? Don't lose heart

It happens to everyone! The best journals have rejection rates of about 70%. Take the criticism, make some changes and send it to another journal.

Starting the search for audiences for your research during your PhD not only gives your thesis the chance of a life-after-submission, but also puts you on the path to post-PhD success and achievement!

And finally ...

Here we end. This is the end of the beginning of the research that will lead to your PhD, and 'Doctor' before your name. Research is an iterative process, frustrating when things go wrong and you can't see your way ahead, but also exhilarating, creative, obsessive and ultimately rewarding.

The road ahead will be dominated by doing it (whatever it is), trying to make sense of the data you generate or insights you gain, writing, rewriting, and rewriting again to get it into a coherent form. Then after it is completed and you turn your mind to other things, you have the viva: the final defence of your research question, how you researched it, what you found and what it means.

That is outside the scope of this little guide. We hope our experiences will prove useful to you as you plan your PhD journey.

References

Clark G (2000). Conversation with Kate Williams, June.

Higher Education Funding Council for England (2007). PhD research degrees: update. Available at www.hefce.ac.uk/Pubs/HEFCE/2007/07_28. [Accessed 5 November 2009]

Kambole M and Struthers P (2009). Attitudes of physiotherapists in Botswana to treating people living with HIV/AIDS. *South African Journal of Physiotherapy*. 65(2) p13–16.

Palmer I (2005). Edge effect and arborial collembola in coniferous plantations. PhD thesis. Roehampton University Library.

Useful sources

Bentley P (2006). *The PhD application handbook.* Maidenhead: Open University Press.

Rugg G and Petre M (2004). *The unwritten rules of PhD research.* Maidenhead: Open University Press.

Thomas G (2009). *How to do your research project.* London: Sage.

Trafford V and Leshem S (2008). *Stepping stones to achieving your doctorate.* Maidenhead: Open University Press.

Wellington J, Bathmaker A, Hunt C, McCulloch G and Sikes P (2005). *Succeeding with your doctorate.* London: Sage.

Useful websites

Research Councils (UK) See www.rcuk.ac.uk:
   AHRC: Arts and Humanities Research Council
   BBSRC: Biotechnology and Biological Sciences Research Council
   EPSRC: Engineering and Physical Sciences Research Council
   ESRC: Economic and Social Research Council
   MRC: Medical Research Council
   NERC: Natural Environment Research Council
   STFC: Science and Technology Facilities Council

Research Excellence Framework: See www.ref.ac.uk
www.findaphd.com
www.jobs.ac.uk
www.scholarship-search.org.uk

And for some light relief: www.phdcomics.com

Index